OPERATION POLICE PSYCHIC

THE DIFFERENT MINDS OF AN OFFICER'S WORLD!

BY:
MARY CALDWELL EVANS

OPERATIONS POLICE PSYCHIC: The different minds of an officer's world.

Copyright © 2021 Mary Caldwell-Evans

All rights reserved. This book or any portion thereof may not be reproduced or used in any manner whatsoever without the express written permission of the author except for the use of brief quotations in a book review. Printed in the United States of America.

First Printing

ISBN- 978-1-955148-11-5 pbk
ISBN- 978-1-955148-12-2 ebk

A2Z Books Publishing Lithonia, GA 30058
www.A2ZBooksPublishing.net
Manufactured in the United States of America.
A2Z Books Publishing has allowed this work to remain exactly as the Publisher & Author Intended.

TABLE OF CONTENTS

ACKNOWLEDGMENTS v
DEDICATION viii
PREFACE ix
OBJECTIVES x
INTRODUCTION 1
SELF-AWARENESS 1
PHASE I 7
ROOKIE EXPERIENCE 8
MY ROOKIE EXPERIENCE 12
YOUR ROOKIE EXPERIENCE 25
      BEHIND THE SCENE 26
      BEHIND YOUR SCENE 28
I CHANGED 29
      YOU'VE CHANGED 32
BELIEFS/CORE VALUES 33
PHASE II 36
"FRIEND OR FOE" 37
"YOUR FRIEND OR FOE" 44

BEHIND THE SCENE	45
BEHIND YOUR SCENE	47
I CHANGED	48
YOU'VE CHANGED	50
BELIEFS/CORE VALUES	51
"WALKING ON SUNSHINE"	56
"MOON LAYING ON YOU"	58
"PUSHING ON"	60
"DRAGGING IN"	62
PHASE III	**64**
CUT MY LOSES	65
WIN OR LOSE	88
BEHIND THE SCENE	89
BEHIND YOUR SCENE	92
I CHANGED	93
YOU'VE CHANGED	97
BELIEFS/CORE VALUES	98
UNDERSTANDING	**101**
CONCLUSION	**102**
NOTES:	105
REFLECTIONS:	108
Reference	110
BIOGRAPHY	**111**
My Prayer:	113

ACKNOWLEDGMENTS

I would like to thank my family. My husband Bobby, our children Robert, Bobby Jr. Myracle and grandson Kendall, you have always been very supportive. Thanks to all of my brothers, sisters, stepbrothers, stepsister, nieces and nephews, for without you all I would not have the practice lessons of life. Special thanks to my sisters Patricia Gillion and Wanda Caldwell, Lisa Banks my childhood friend and Derrick Jennings friend of the family all are avid readers and great supporters.

Thanks to Big Brother Jimmy Gillion and my Sister-in-law Cynthia Gillion without you I would not have gotten my Bachelor's Degree. Thanks to Dale Lane, you continued to encourage me to go to Graduate School. Thanks to Alicia Hill for taking a personal interest in my endeavor. Thanks to my partner and dear friend, Clarence Turks who had my back and his wife Mrs. Vickie who allowed us to be friends as she became my friend also, a very special lady. Thanks to Keisha Scott, you pushed me to apply for Deputy Sheriff and always pushed me to be a better shooter and it paid off. Thanks to Eriq and Ola Jordan. Thanks to Gary Myles @ MYLESAPARTPHOTOGRAPHY.COM. Thanks to Dr. Richard Harrell Jr. Thanks to Pastor Perry Maples Jr. for spiritual guidance. Thank you to my editor, high school classmate and friend, Adrienne Williams.

Very special thanks to the one and only Mom (Pairlee Caldwell Gillion). The example you have lived before us has given me more than any textbook could ever teach. Thank you for the wisdom, prayers, strength, accountability, determination and fear of God that has molded my life solid. You have been the best example of a mother and grandmother in this old world.

My mother had eleven children and she did not have much time for unnecessary details. All she wanted to know was what happened, who was there and what did you do? After further investigation with all parties involved, she ruled. This was the type of example I have had before me all of my life. Nothing in life seemed to unravel her. She made decisions without prejudice or bias and some decisions were very critical.

She would always say, "Baby common sense ain't common no more." Meaning everybody do not think logically nor does making good decisions come naturally easy for them. Mom taught us problem-solving skills very early in our childhood. We learned how to solve or resolve problems between ourselves. When we involved Mom, sometimes her decisions punished everybody. She punished the one that came and told her, the one that was told on and the others for not stopping it. So then, we would come together and make a consensus, some thought it was a fair outcome and some did not. The common goal was to work it out the best way we could and not involve her.

My oldest sister Barbara was the Commanding General when Mom was gone and we all understood her authority. She did not rule with an iron fist like Mom but she had a heavy hand just the same. She was murdered in May 1976 and left five small children. Her ex-boyfriend was a fatal attraction. He said if I can't have you nobody can. Mom and my stepfather kept my little nieces and nephews together and raised them with the rest of us. Other family members offered to take some of them, but they refused.

They kept all five of my sister's children plus the ten of us without a second thought. You talk about making critical decisions and grieving at the same time. If they had split us up it would have been another family tragedy.

My sister Beatrice was murdered in February of 1983. She had four small children. My parents brought their four little grandchildren home to Memphis, TN and we lived on together.

I remember when my brother Herbert was murdered. You were questioning yourself as to where you went wrong. I told you to stop it because you had given all of your children and grandchildren everything you had. I realized at that moment that the burden a mother carries for her children is a life sentence. You told me something that I try to continue to do.

You said, "in bad times always find a reason to laugh." We have been so blessed to have you. These are some of the examples of the kind of strength I grew up in. Words cannot express the love you have sown into our lives. Just saying thank you is not enough but THANK YOU, I owe you everything and I LOVE YOU DEEPLY MOM.

DEDICATION

I dedicate this Book to our **FIRST RESPONDERS and MILITARY**.

Where would this Country be without our First Responders and Military? We depend on them for more than just protection. We depend on them for all sorts of resources, medication, information, collaboration, mediation, and services. It takes special people, made up in a certain way to cope with the stress and pressures of these jobs on a daily basis, night and day, without falling apart.

Hats off to the incredible people of first responders, military, doctors, nurses, police, jailers, fire fighters, paramedics, and all of the essential workers that work behind the scene of these professions, you are all worthy of more respect and better compensation.

We do not defund the police we FUND training, better private discrete mental health assistance, incentives, and better retirement plans!

PREFACE

On August 31, 2019, after 25 years of service, I retired from the Shelby County Sheriff's Office. I was 32 years old when I finally became a Deputy Sheriff. I use the word "finally" because that is not how I started my career. I started as a Data Entry Clerk for two and a half years and then as a Deputy Jailer for eight months. At the time, little did I know that law enforcement fitted my personality like hands in gloves! My personality has exemplified this role all my life.

The most difficult experience about this job was remaining true to self. I am certain that the family sees changes happening but cannot quite put their finger on it. Over the years, this job can and will make or break you. Please make up your mind that you will keep your integrity, ethics, dignity and self-respect. Therefore, make the necessary mindset adjustments to operate on your own psychic and strengthen your inner being to not be consumed. I have had to adjust and re-adjust my mindset to survive many encounters throughout my tenure and you will too.

OBJECTIVES

I am not a doctor of any kind or a therapist. I am just someone who has experienced the life of an officer and made it through successfully. When I say successfully, I mean I did not turn to destructive coping tools and I did not compromise my integrity and core beliefs. I was an Instructor at the Training Academy for four years. I taught all levels of law enforcement officers and I know that we are more comfortable working our problems out alone than sharing them in a classroom setting. This book works better by looking at yourself more candidly and finding what changes work best for you.

- ✓ **Change Self**
- ✓ **Change an Officer**
- ✓ **Change a Precinct**
- ✓ **Change a Division**
- ✓ **Change a Department**
- ✓ **Change an Administration**
- ✓ **Change a City one at a time**.

This is why I created a self-help book for you, my fellow law enforcement officers. It is to assist you in balancing, coping, healing within and without throughout your career. Sometimes, writing down your feelings and thoughts are therapeutic. I have given you some insight into who I am and why I think the way I do. I want to put this police life in perspective so you can understand and recognize what is happening in the phases of your career. The incidences may not have happened to you but I know beyond a shadow of a doubt that you can relate to this book in many ways. Trust me, these things have happened in departments somewhere and even worse has happened!

Transparency is how you get the best results from this book.

The objectives are to help officers recognize the phases of their career and also understand the changes that are happening to them simultaneously in those phases. This brings awareness to them so they may know that the changes are necessary and healthy, but the right changes are the challenge. You should already have boundaries in your life knowing who you are and what is right and wrong before you became a police. Take an honest look at yourself to see how far you have drifted from that person you were before you started.

I have written this in three phases:

1). WHY do I do this job?

The Rookie Phase is first. Depending on the size of the city and the volume of crime, one to five years span is what I consider a Rookie. Most Rookies come on the job with the attitude that this is my calling. This is what I have always wanted to do all of my life. The most important of all is I want to make a difference in this world and help people. All of these reasons are admirable and really good reasons. Through your Rookie years, if nothing traumatic has happened, trust me it is bound to happen in these next five to twenty years.

2). WHAT in the world am I doing this job for?

The second phase is Friend or Foe. These are the years that can make or break you. Even in the mistakes you make (and you are going to make them), you become a friend or foe to the public and within the department. It depends on who you know, who knows you, who likes you, who doesn't like you, who owes you, or if you are willing to return a favor if they help you, whether you come out with a friend or foe or not. Then you begin to ask yourself, **what in the world am I doing this job for?**

3). How much longer can I do this job?

The third phase is Win or Lose. After spending more than twenty years on the job, you start to analyze your tenure. Have I been promoted or not? Why haven't I gotten promoted? What have I accomplished or not? Then after you have answered these questions, you may have no desire to go to any specialized units, unless at this point it is less work, depending on your health. You wonder when can I get out of here, draw my retirement and do something else to be financially comfortable, if I need to.

I knew an officer that quit. He had about seven years left and the administration talked him into staying until his full retirement. Of course, most of us are not that fortunate. I have known officers to retire in eighteen, twenty years right at the door of full retirement, but they just could not do it anymore. **How much longer can I do this job?**

Have you changed since you started?

_____

_____

_____

_____

_____

INTRODUCTION

SELF-AWARENESS

My biggest enemy is in me! As law enforcement officers, we must be honest with ourselves. This is the beginning of self-growth and healing. Anything that does not grow eventually fades away. Change is uncomfortable but necessary. It is very easy to become comfortable in bad behavior until it is exposed before the world and at that point, we will be shamed. When we become officers, our character flaws do not disappear. With more in depth ethics training, officers can understand themselves in order to make decisions without prejudices and biases.

Ethics is the bedrock of law enforcement. So why has ethics training dwindled to officers watching a thirty-minute video and signing the list that they have watched it? This is just unacceptable when this job is submerged in ethics, integrity, core values, beliefs, judgment and decision making every day. The decisions officers make – whether personal or professional – comes from what they know and believe. Therefore, the ethics program in law enforcement is the foundation in training.

Mistakes in life are made, which is expected. Officers have insecurities because we are human. We certainly do not want to make these mistakes because we are experiencing our own personal breaking point. Also, officers make mistakes because we do not know when to apply what we know; and yeah sometimes we just have officers with no integrity. Written rules tell what behavior is wrong or right. Our moral principles personally convict and alert us to what we believe is wrong or right. Life experiences make us witnesses to what we know and education enlightens us to what someone else wants us to know. Trust me, the core person of who you are – good or bad – will be discovered in this job and sometimes, the whole world sees you. I do not want you to be next!

Officers will tell you that in this job, timing is everything in most cases. For example, something as simple as being able to draw your weapon in three seconds or less can save your life. Administering CPR on someone as soon as possible can save a life. Knowing when it is time to fight or flight can save your life. Responding as quickly as you can to an active shooting can save more lives. These are just a few examples of how important timing is in this career.

Please just follow me, I am trying to make a point. Everyone needs to know the time for some reason; to get up in the morning, get the children to school and go to work. You need to know the time to catch a flight for an important meeting. You need to know the deadline of business transactions or release dates. You even take medication at certain times of the day. When you go to the doctor, he/she may ask you, "when was the first time you noticed you had a fever?"

If you go to a mental health facility, the doctor will ask you when the first time you start thinking about suicide. Even the homeless people need to know what time the shelter opens and when to get food. It is time to change the oil in the vehicle, change the filter in the furnace, and time to cut the grass. Therefore, everyone needs to know the "Time" - black, white, red, yellow, rich, poor and all in between.

As I said before, I am not a doctor or therapist of any kind. I do not have the answers to your problems. I cannot speak for anyone but myself from my point of view about my career as a Law Enforcement Officer. But I do know that:

"The most honest thing you can tell yourself in the course of your career is Time."

We must not just live our lives as though we have no control over the outcome of it and most of us do not. On the other hand, we should make time to analyze our life just like doctors do when they are trying to figure out why we are sick. Most police officers I know are very analytical so this should be easy, right? All of us discover hard facts about ourselves if we are brutally honest. One thing you cannot do is bull-shit officers because we are the best at it and we learn people.

I was teaching Critical Thinking for Law Enforcement at the training academy which is a curriculum that I created. One of the questions in the Core Values/Beliefs section was, "What is your weakness?"

Sidebar: This curriculum was created because of an episode in the department. There was an officer that pulled over an SUV for speeding. The driver was taking his elderly mother to the emergency room. The hospital was about two minutes away from where they were stopped. The officer called for an ambulance instead of allowing the driver to continue to the hospital. The driver's elderly mother passed away in the back seat of the SUV. Some encounters for officers are not in policy and procedure; just **human compassion and common sense!** *I cannot beat this dead horse enough, know yourself! The Sheriff came to the training academy and had a meeting with the staff and said; "I need you to come up with some kind of curriculum to teach the officers common sense; you cannot call it that but that's what it is." So, I went to work on it.*

Ok back to the incident, an officer responded loudly in class, "I don't have a weakness," and my response to him was, "Please, give me your wife's number I bet she could tell me ten of them off the top of her head." He got so angry with me, and then I said to him, "I see one of your weaknesses right now." Over time, officers become jaded, cenacle, insensitive and our sense of humor grows a little warped. We tend to laugh at things that would not be funny to the public. If we are brutally honest, we would know what time it is in our lives but we are pros at hiding behind that badge. The badge gives us power, authority and control over others so we can deflect our behavior in so many ways.

As police officers, we have to keep checking our behavior. Because making decisions every day on how we handle the bad behaviors of others can cause stress on how we cope with our own behavior. I call this **"Hard to Heart Time."** In other words, over time, have you changed so much until you can no longer do your job with the same concern, attitude and disposition you had when you started?

You should begin to evaluate your behavior by asking yourself these questions:

a) At what time in my career did I start thinking this way?

b) What happened to make me think like this?

c) When was the first thought?

d) How often do I think about it?

POLICE

Perceptions-Overseeing-Lives-Involving-Contact-Enforcement

Head = Heart - *People can be deceiving and you can deceive yourself.*

411 vs 911 - *Does the information given conflict with what you are looking at in real-time?*

Time vs Decision — *On the scene, we have seconds to make good decisions.*

Law Enforcement + People — *The people need us and we need the people.*

THE BALANCE OF LIFE

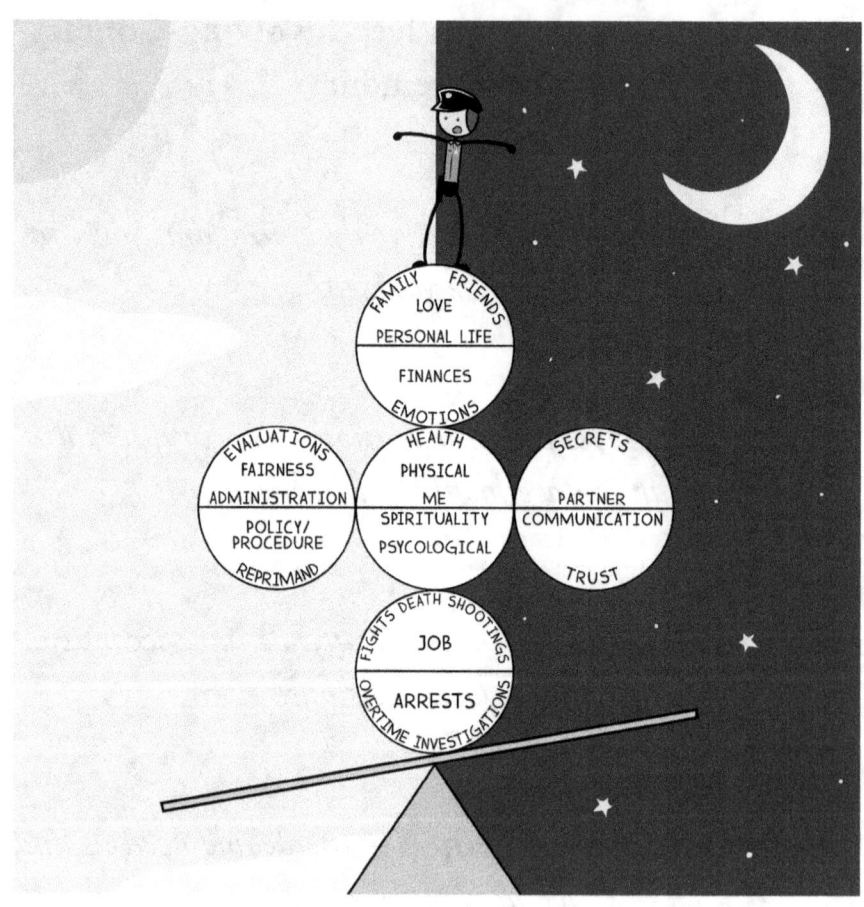

PHASE I

ROOKIE EXPERIENCE

WHY do we do this job?

At the Rookie Phase, you feel that you are invincible. I was Instructing a Recruit Class. I said to the class some days you will not feel 100 percent. One of the Recruits said Ma'am, I feel 110% every day. Then I ask him how old are you? He said 28 years old Ma'am. My response to him was "keep living."

Police Officers see and deal with the invisible forces of good and evil that operates in people every day. I think we all start out with the same intentions to help, to make a difference in people's lives no matter how small. There is something self-fulfilling about serving mankind for the greater good. We understand we fight the bad and protect the good in society. I also know that over time, that spark in our hearts for the greater good can be tarnished, bruised, darkened and sometimes put out.

Why do you do this policing job?

_____
_____
_____
_____
_____
_____

This uniform tells people that we are **The Public's Information Center.** People ask us for directions. I have had people ask me, what is a good restaurant in the city to take their family? Who serves the best BBQ in Memphis?

Other times, we are **Psychiatrists.** People tell us about their most personal lives and expect advice. A young man flagged me down one day in my squad car. He asked me if I could follow him to the apartment to retrieve his belongings. I told him that it is a civil matter and since his female companion was not at home we cannot go into her apartment.

He went on to tell me that she has a fifteen-year-old son that lives with them. He explained how disrespectful the teenager is to him and especially to his mother. Then he said, "I don't think our relationship is going to make it." I said how so? He said, "she allows her fifteen-year-old teenage son to walk around the house nude in front of her."

He also said, "He is well endowed (large penis) even more than me." Well, I kept a straight face; I was not expecting to hear that. Needless to say, after he made that comment, we talked for at least thirty more minutes. Sometimes people feel better telling a total stranger (officer) their innermost feelings. I do not know why, I guess they feel safe.

Share some crazy personal information people have shared with you while confiding in you.

_____

_____

_____

_____

_____

We are F**amily and Marriage Counselors.** We know domestic violence calls are one of the most dangerous for officers. We get on the scene and try to sort out what is really going on. The wife is screaming and the husband or significant other is ranting and raving. Sometimes, the wife is all beat up and the husband is holding the children hostage at gun point threatening to kill himself and everybody. So, we have to strategize to try and save everyone but we all know it does not always turn out for the best. Sometimes the scenes are not so bad and sometimes they are worse than expected.

We are the **Intervention Team.** Some of the things children suffer at the hand of their parents or guardian are horrendous. Officers try to call help centers to place our children.

We are **Humanitarians.** Drug addicts and homeless people have been in the streets for so many years until we get to know them. We buy them a cup of coffee or something to eat trying to provide a little human comfort for a moment. Depending on how bad these homeless people become, we have to call other agencies to help them and sometimes they do not want help.

The **Crisis Intervention** team assists with mental illness calls and these can be very dangerous. Sometimes being familiar with the person is good and sometimes bad. We have been to so many calls about the same person in crisis until we get familiar. We do not like to get so familiar with the person until we let our guards down.

Give some experiences of being a public servant in the field.
_____
_____
_____
_____
_____

We encounter interviews and arrest different kinds of robbers, rapists, murderers, and attempted murderers on the job. We have gang members;

gang violence is so prevalent in our communities to combat. Everyone we come in contact with or arrest has friends and family concerned about them. We deal with people that have been victimized. We talk to the friends and family of the victims.

Oh, did I mention the immediate Supervisor and Administration have expectations of what they want us to do? For example, how many tickets they want you to write in a day's work or how many arrests if you work in the Fugitive Division? Of course, they say we cannot make these expectations mandatory but we know they want it done.

Note to self: I have my own life and personal problems to deal with at home too. I mean it seems as though after four to five years, you question your perspectives. The "why" to us often becomes foggy when dealing with the administration's bureaucracy and our partners along with the people we serve every day, OMG!

Have you realized that the reason you became an officer has changed? When and Why?

_____

_____

_____

_____

_____

_____

_____

_____

MY ROOKIE EXPERIENCE

Deputy Jailer

On my first official day, I was assigned to the women's side of the jail and at that time they were all still in the same building with the male inmates. Sergeant Nonchalant told officer Burnout to train Officer Evans. It was 06:00 that morning and she said okay. After Sergeant Nonchalant left, officer Burnout said, "I am not training anybody." She gave me the pod keys – the keys that open the cells where the incarcerated live.

I said to myself alright Mary; you are on your own. Eventually, it was the inmates that taught me what to do that morning. When the officer returned at the end of the shift, I had finished all my duties. The inmates had taken turns taking showers, cleaning up their cells, and completing daily duties. Officer Burnout was very surprised. We became the best of co-workers. You see, I could not trust her totally but I could trust her to the extent that we could work together and get along. I could have become bitter and revengeful but I did not.

Officer Burnout began to tell me every time they get someone new that she had to train them. She was not being compensated for training. She felt like they were taking advantage of her. Sometimes, it is good to put yourself in someone else's position before you render a judgment. So yeah, I understood her frustration but Officer Burnout did not realize she was changing.

Recall a time when an officer was burnout, their morale was low, and they took it out on you?

_____

_____

_____

_____

Were you understanding towards them? What could you have done to make things a little lighter for them?

_____

_____

_____

_____

The first time I heard those iron doors slam behind me and I knew that I could not get out unless someone pushed a button to let me out, this was a dreadful feeling. However, once you go in and out every day you get used to it. It is amazing what the human mind can adapt to.

Share how you felt on your first official day working in the jail. Did you notice when you forgot about the fear of the iron doors slamming behind you?

_____

_____

_____

_____

_____

_____

_____

Establishing Boundaries

I was working on the third or fourth-floor adult male pod. The inmates called me a black bitch every day; you must think you are the real police you ain't nothin but a turn-key, they would say. I didn't care about that. I was just really trying to learn my job and do my job. I was fair, firm and consistent and they did not like it at first. They started with the intimidation tactics. They were trying to find a weakness in me. Inmates are the best psychiatrists and psychologists I know without a degree. If you have never worked in the jail, all I can tell you is it is a different world. It is for the big men and women; you must have a strong inner being to survive and retire.

I was alone in an elevator with an inmate. He was very attractive. He said you are the one that thinks you are the real police. He said don't go around here making enemies. I responded, I am not here to make friends either. He was testing me and you have to have a comeback to establish your boundaries, yes even with inmates. We looked at each other in the eyes and he knew that I was not easy prey or afraid of him.

I know you have heard of officers having sex with the inmates or bringing them contraband in the jail, and you think how could they do something so stupid? If you do not have your mind wrapped tightly in that environment while coming in every single day, the inmates will get you. The inmates are like lions and bears seeking prey. They can catch you on one of those low days because they are always watching and waiting; that's all they have to do all day. They are so cunning and crafty that over time it can happen, has happened and will continue to happen; we would like to minimize that percentage of our officers failing.

Name some officers you knew were not cut out for the job? Did they get in some kind of trouble with the inmates? What did they do? Did you warn them? Did you learn from their mistake?

_____
_____
_____
_____
_____
_____
_____
_____
_____
_____
_____

I was moved to the P Building. This was while the female jail was being built in the 1990s. Sargent Shakkey was my supervisor. She called me into the Control Center. The Control Center is surrounded by glass, where most of the buttons are located to let you in and out of the inmates' dorms. Officers observe what is going on through the glass.

I stepped into the Control Center and an inmate was in there; this was a no-no, but I did not say a word about that at the time. Sgt. Shakkey said inmate Crafty said you are picking on her. She said every time she needs something, you won't help her but you help everybody else. So, I listened to the Sarge tell me all of inmate Crafty's accusations.

Then I said to Sgt. Shakkey, inmate Crafty and her Celly (friend in jail) told me from day one they run the dorm; they tell the inmates what to do around here. Therefore, I have to tell inmate Crafty every day that this is my dorm and I run it from 06:00-02:00. I don't care what they do when I'm not here. So this has caused tension and friction between us. No Ma'am, I don't pick on her, I don't care enough about her to pick on her. I don't think about her, I don't have her on my mind when I leave this place. I am just trying to do my job.

Inmate Crafty started crying. I mean, she boo-hoo-boo-hoo so loudly. She caught us off guard that was so unexpected. She said, I have five children and I have not seen them. I miss my children. Sgt. Shakkey and I looked at each other in amazement. I got up from my chair and walked out of the Control Center. I continued to write up inmate Crafty until they gave her some days in the hole. I guess I'm like my Mother, I just don't do foolishness.

I respectfully said something to Sgt. Shakkey about the way she handled that situation. It took a little while but we finally worked it out and got alone.

Name some supervisors that took the inmate's word over yours in your presence. How did it make you feel? How did you handle it? Did you change?

_____
_____
_____
_____
_____
_____
_____
_____
_____
_____
_____
_____
_____

Sidebar: In my opinion, officers that have worked in the jail are better officers in the street (to some degree-most of the time), especially when it comes to dealing with criminals, compared to officers that have never worked with a criminal mindset in any way. That is not to say that there are no good officers in the street that do not have that experience.

But I say this because you learn the behavior and mindset of criminals in a personal and intimate way. This is nothing that you can learn from a textbook, this must be experienced. Also, you learn diplomacy when dealing with inmates because you are outnumbered and locked up in there with them. You learn how to talk to them and respect them – whether you like them or not. You will learn how to get them to do what you want them to do without fighting every day. If you think you are going in there to kick ass and take names, you won't last. You will come to work with your old wounds and a fresh inmate ready to fight. You will learn how to get your job done without bullying and confrontation. You will learn how to respect the men and women that are incarcerated. <u>Remember this is just my opinion!</u>

I had a heated discussion with Officer Howdy. We worked at the academy together. At the time, the Sheriff's Department was giving the Jailers a big bump-up in pay. I said, "It's about time they deserve it." He said, "I don't think they do." I asked him, "Have you ever worked in jail?" He said, no. I said, "How can you even have an opinion on something you know nothing about? It is not an opinion; it's just the way you feel about something that you don't understand." So I told him until you work locked up with criminals all day and night, I don't want to hear it. He replied, "If I had to work in that jail, I will quit first." I responded, so why are you so against the Jailer receiving their money? After all, it is not coming out of your pocket and somebody's got to do the job. So needless to say, I was on ten at this point.

Deputy Sheriff

Establishing Boundaries

Some officers already come with ill intentions but do not let them change you. You are still responsible to enforce the law by obeying it first. My partner and I disagreed about how to do our job in the streets. He said, I can't ride with you. I said okay. He said, I am going to tell Sarge when we get in tonight that I can't ride with you. I said okay you can tell him whatever you want to tell him.

I am not going to the bus stop of approximately 30 black people to check their IDs for warrants. It was 05:00 pm and these people were waiting for the bus to go home after a hard day's work. We never rode together in a squad car as partners again. This Deputy and I were recruits at the same time and we graduated from the academy together. I was labeled as a radical and a Yankee.

Lieutenant Middleman had roll call and gave direct orders to stop calling me that. Actually, that did not bother me. I was raised in a very large family and I grew up in the inner city of St. Louis, MO. I was not sensitive. I think it bothered someone else.

Share a crucial time in your career when you had to make a judgment call against your partner or fellow officer. Were you ridiculed for it? How did it make you feel at that time? If you had to do it all over again would you do it the same way? What did you learn from that experience?

_____

_____

_____

_____

The first pivotal incident that changed my heart towards my career as a deputy Sheriff happened when I worked in Fugitive Transport. The Deputy Jailers had been responsible for transporting inmates back and forth to medical facilities for health care for so many years, as long as I could remember. For some reason, the Sheriff decided to give the law enforcement officers Deputy Sheriff's Fugitive Transport duties.

It was morning and like any other day, we went to roll call then got the squad car keys and equipment, handcuffs, and shackles. We all drove around into the sally port which is where we all parked the vehicles and go inside the jail to get the inmates. None of us really wanted to go inside the jail so we were all standing around the sally port waiting to see who would volunteer to get the inmates.

Before we knew it, Officer Saucy (male white) walks across the sally port and points his finger directly down into Officer Pepper's (female black) face. He said in a very angry voice after all I have done for you; I came over to your house and fixed your car. All of us were stunned. We had no idea that these two officers even socialize outside of the workplace. Officer Pepper just stood there looking up at him.

Did I mention that Officer Saucy's father was a Chief in the Sheriff's Department? This was one of those moments I wished I could have disappeared. Of course, the Sheriff's Department opened an internal investigation. Every officer was called in at some point to give a statement as to what they witnessed.

I was at the hospital's holding area watching the inmates. The phone rang and it was for me. I answered the phone and Lieutenant Middleman informed me that I knew what to say when I gave my statement. If I wanted my job, I knew what to say. He said, back in the day you would have come up missing. We would threaten to do something to your family but I know it won't come to that.

After Lt. Middleman finished threatening me, he said do you hear me? I said, Yes Sir. I asked him if he was finished and he said yeah and I slammed the phone down. I was angry and astonished at the same time, that something like this was still going on. This conversation changed my total image of the entire sheriff's department. I became detached from the comradely of the job. It was so bad that I had to reprogram my mindset to continue to work.

After a crucial incident in your career tarnished the way you felt about the department, how did you cope? How many years had you been an officer?

_____

_____

_____

_____

_____

_____

_____

_____

I did not tell a soul about the phone call; first of all, I couldn't believe it. I most certainly didn't think anyone else would believe it. I did not tell my husband or anyone in the family; there was no need to alarm them. They could not help me anyway. I told one close friend. I had to tell someone I could trust that would believe me. She said what are you going to do? I said nothing. What can I do? I can't prove it. He called me from the fugitive office at the hospital. The phone numbers on the caller ID shows the generic main number. Plus, phone calls come from the office to the hospital all day does not prove anything.

No one else heard the call, so I would sound crazy to say that Lt. Middleman threatened me. So, I had to let it go but it planted a seed I needed of paranoia and distrust. I had only been an officer for about four years when this happened. I began to change little by little without knowing it. It just kind of sneaks up on you.

Sidebar: Lieutenant Middleman and I became friends after he retired. I saw him years later and we laughed about how I shot out the windshield in my car. He said, when you called me I was on my riding mower cutting the grass. I said, you what? Then he said, Mary, I am a Christian now and have found Jesus and I am not the same man. I embraced him. Every now and then we call each other to catch up on family.

When they called me into the office to give my statement, I was so nervous. I did not know what to expect because this was my first time giving a statement in an internal investigation. I sat in the waiting area and prayed hard, I mean extremely hard. I said, Dear Lord, give me the words to say. Please let me say only what I need to say and nothing more. Give me the strength to tell the truth, in Jesus Name Amen.

I went into the questioning room. Director Spade asked me, what happened? Then, Director Spade said let me show you the video of the incident first. I was thinking to myself, you have the video so you do not need my testimony. He played the video and as Officer Saucy starts walking across the sally port towards Officer Pepper; the television snowed out. I could not see a thing.

When did you give your first statement in an internal investigation?

_____

_____

_____

_____

_____

_____

My heart dropped. I could not believe they were playing this game about something so serious. I sat there for some seconds but, it felt like minutes. I did not say anything. My mind was racing; is this a trick question or something? Ain't this some shit? What in the world. I was praying in my mind too; God, what do I say after these shenanigans? These people are crazier than I thought.

Then, that voice as clear as the blue skies on a sunny day said, "tell the truth." So I said, I am going to tell you the truth and you can do whatever you want to do with it. So yes, I told them exactly what I saw and heard happened between deputies Peppers and Saucy. After I gave my statement I could see Director Spade's reaction. He had this look on his face…huh, she told the truth.

I believe officers get fired from this job for truthfulness more than any other reasons. Also, they already knew what happened but if I had lied, they could and would have used it against me in the future. You see that is just how this works.

Plus this established my reputation as being honest no matter what the consequences. This job has a way of testing your courage, inner-self, boundaries, beliefs, and core values.

When your back was against the wall did you tell the truth? Did you regret your statement? Why or why not?

_____

_____

_____

_____

_____

YOUR ROOKIE EXPERIENCE

Rookie Picture

BEHIND THE SCENE

I remembered the time of this incident so vividly because my daughter was born in August of 2000. I returned to work somewhere around the first of 2001. This is when I experienced my very first migraine headache. I was sitting with an inmate in the hospital when my head began to pound so badly until my eyes became sensitive to the light. I could not open my eyes. I was nauseous but could not throw up. I called the inmate holding area to ask someone to relieve me so I could walk around to the emergency room.

I held on to the wall while walking around to the emergency room. I thought I had a tumor or something. You know we always think the worse. So, the doctor checked me out from head to toe and could not find anything. He was a wise old doctor. He said, what is going on in your life? What has recently changed for you? I could not think of anything.

Then I said oh yeah, I work the night shift and I know that I'm not getting enough sleep due to the fact that I have a baby and she's about five months old. I have been working lots of overtime too. He said, you are under stress – you are stressed out. He gave me some days off work. Then he said, your migraine should go away. If you don't make some lifestyle changes you will have more. The days off work were good but it was cutting into my overtime. On the other hand, it gave me time to think about my life and what was truly important to me. I have never had another migraine headache in my life, so that should answer your question as to what I decided to do.

I set limited hours a week to work overtime and that was it. I spent quality time at home with my three children. My oldest son was a junior in high school. It was time to get him ready for graduation and college. I sent him off to college with everything he needed. My baby boy was getting ready for middle school and this was also a special transition experience in his life.

My marriage was on thin ice and the baby was unexpected. Of course, she was nevertheless the love of my life. Time is more precious than money. I still made more money than I had ever made in my life working in Fugitive Transport that year. I am certain it was true for other officers at that time.

Share a time you worked so much overtime until you were too tired to spend the money?

_____

_____

_____

_____

_____

_____

BEHIND YOUR SCENE

I CHANGED

When my WHY changed, everything else changed too.

Can you imagine all of this was going on in my personal life simultaneously during the internal investigation? Yes, I was stressed out! The choice I made to be home more and put my family first was easier to make after the phone call from Lt. Middleman. The job became my livelihood and not my life.

When did you have that aha moment to reassess your priorities?

_____

_____

_____

_____

I am describing in detail the chain of events in my life. As an officer, my decisions that eventually led me from point A to point B to point C in this career. This job changes us. I don't care how we say that it does not; we change regardless. We have to change just to survive. As officers, we learn very quickly the dos and don'ts. We do not volunteer information only answer what is asked. Do not show your weaknesses or fears. I was an instructor at the Training Academy for four years and I know that is why I decided to make a self-help book.

We try for the most part not to take our job home. Sometimes it is hard to do, especially if it's on television, radio and social media. This kind of job affects us in ways we do not realize until years later and we don't talk about it. I hope and pray that this book will help you realize the changes in you and in your life. **That's not to say that all of the changes are bad because they are not.**

After working in the streets for so long you learn people's behavior; it is inevitable. I think this is a good quality to have. We tend to think that if we are not the police, then nobody else understands us. We discover our fears and weaknesses in the streets. I am very afraid of dogs and that was magnified working in the streets. I became paranoid (not the unhealthy kind), nevertheless, more paranoid than if I had not been a police.

After becoming an officer, share something you do now that you did not do before? Why?

Some officers cannot handle the power and authority over people. Treat people with respect. That's the key unless they choose otherwise. I worked in drug court with Deputy Bonderson. The judge would lock those dope dealing boys up just about every other day. They would take that bank roll of money in a rubber band and give it to their attorney and say "get me out of here!" It seemed like Deputy Bonderson would get so angry at those dope boys. He would grab'em, rough'em up, push their faces against the wall, and pulled their pants up hard in their groin.

We were scuffling with them every other day or so. So I pulled Deputy Bonderson to the side and had a one on one. I told him you are too prejudiced to work in this courtroom. I am not going to be fighting and scuffling every other day because you are prejudiced. You need to request a transfer anywhere but somewhere else from here. About two weeks later he was transferred. Deputy Bonderson saw me about five years later and said thank you. You were right, I just couldn't handle it but he did not thank me at the time I told him.

Have you abused your power and authority? Why and did you stop?

_____
_____
_____
_____
_____
_____

When officers are involved in a shooting of any kind, fight or flight situation in most instances, it changes our lives in some way.

Share a fight or flight incident that changed your life and how are you different because of it? Do you think you are a better person or worse? Ask your family and close friends.

_____
_____
_____
_____
_____
_____

YOU'VE CHANGED

Police-Efficacy – Has experiences on the job affected you and your ability to be effective in the field?

_____
_____
_____
_____
_____
_____
_____
_____
_____
_____
_____
_____
_____
_____
_____
_____
_____
_____
_____
_____

BELIEFS/CORE VALUES

I ask you these questions because I believe honest self-evaluation strengthens self-identification. It is very easy to see what you did but, in some instances, it is more difficult to explain why you did it. The naked eye cannot see motive in action. Motive has to be explained or discovered. I want you to assess yourself from beliefs/core values to understand who you are but most importantly, why you are that way. As the phases in your career change, you change also. I want to help you identify the different phases and recognize how they have changed you and why you made those changes. **If my experiences can help one officer live the best life in this career, I would have accomplished my mission.**

1) What motivates you? Why?

_____

_____

_____

_____

_____

2) What makes you get up every day and do the police thing?

_____

_____

_____

_____

_____

3) What is right and wrong to you? Explain yourself.

_____
_____
_____
_____
_____
_____
_____

4) Is preserving life more important to you than anything else and how do you know?

_____
_____
_____
_____
_____
_____
_____

5) Do you hate the bad guy or do you hate what they do or both? Explain yourself and give an example.

PHASE II

"FRIEND OR FOE"

As years pass, the "Why I do this job," becomes WHAT in the world am I doing this job for?

This is the longest part of your career. It is more than likely the stage you may get promoted. You may finally get a bid or transfer into a specialized unit you have been waiting to do, for example, S.W.A.T. or Detective Division. If you do not get that exact position, then you take your second or third option. You begin to feel a little excited, confident and capable in your duties as you learn something new.

This is also where it can get slightly tricky. This job is not concrete; it is very fluid and this leaves officers vulnerable to mistakes on a daily basis. On any scene, officers know things can go from zero to ten in a split second. It does not have to be a crisis call. You come to a house to serve a simple Civil Warrant and get into a fight with a teenager in the house. An officer has a deadly crash speeding not going to a call, with no blue lights and sirens, this is trouble. If you shoot someone's unleashed dog, it's almost like shooting their child nowadays. We can become friends or enemies to the public and within the department.

Your Sergeant tells you to do a well check on an officer because she was a no call no show to work that night. When you get to her house, a supervisor's unmarked vehicle is in her driveway and she has a restraining order on him. You can easily become a friend or foe depending on what you do and who you tell.

The Officer calls for a Whisky Unit because he thinks someone is Driving Under the Influence (DUI). The suspect makes it home and goes into the house. The Sergeant gets to the scene and the man comes out of the house. The Sergeant wants the Whisky Unit to perform the Blood Alcohol Concentration (BAC) test anyway.

The Officer tells the Sergeant we cannot do that. He is not in the vehicle so we cannot charge him with DUI. The Sergeant gets upset with the Officer and calls the Lieutenant who also calls the Chief. The Officer is transferred to the Midnight Shift effective immediately. An incident like this can bring upon you serious consequences and stress. There are so many crazy examples and I could give more, but you already know. At this point in your career, you change even more. I know you do what you have to do in order to survive and continue the job.

You remember life has happened. You have probably gotten married, a family, a mortgage, cars, children, and your life is wrapped in personal responsibilities and obligations.

Once your why changes, the reason you are committed to the job changes also. Especially, if you have been in a life-changing experience for example a shooting or a fight situation. This is not a bad place to be in your career. In most cases, officers have come to a reckoning and developed a balance in the job and their personal life. You should have begun to spend more time with the family without other police families invited.

You should get involved in your faith-based community, coach little league, volunteer, get on your alumni baseball team, play in the band, etc. This is the therapy for dealing with all of the stress and pressures of the job. You should become more committed to your family obligations and that's okay. We can do the job now without the glorified idea of making a difference in the world. If we make a difference in someone's life, that's a great thing. If we just simply do a good job and go home at the end of the shift that would be alright too.

During the period of "what in the world am I doing this job for," I think at this point your identity of who you are becomes more defined. The why I do this job is not so important.

Define the crossroad in your career? What happened?

_____
_____
_____
_____
_____
_____
_____
_____
_____
_____

The second crucial incident in my career happened in this phase. This was the absolute worst experience of all in my life in the department. I was an instructor at the training academy. Lieutenant Entitlement had a meeting with officer Howdy and me. He encouraged us to go to school. He said if you ever wanted to go to school, this would be a good time; we can work with your schedule. So I started school in September 2009 working on my Bachelor's Degree. Sergeant Dogood was my immediate supervisor. He allowed me to choose my days to teach around my school schedule, no problem.

Sgt. Dogood informed us he was being transferred. I told him that Lt. Entitlement was going to get me when you leave. Sgt. Dogood got transferred in February 2011 and all hell broke loose on me. Sgt. Naïve took his place and I knew his personality was not strong enough to handle Lt. Entitlement.

Name some of your supervisors who did not have a strong constitution to handle conflict between their superiors, officers, and clerical staff. How did you handle the situation?

_____
_____
_____
_____
_____
_____
_____
_____

Lt. Entitlement started doing little things such as keeping up with my every move. I called him and told him I was on the way. I had to drop my daughter off at school. I got to work at 08:00 am. As Soon as I stepped into the lobby of the Academy, he began yelling at me in front of everyone. He said, you are late for work! I said no I'm not. He yelled yes you are! I told you to be here at 07:45! I said yes sir, you did but technically I am not late until after 08:00 am. I do not get paid for those extra 15 minutes. That did not go over well but he could not write me up for being late.

There were other things such as winking his eye at me. He gave me a hard time with my school schedule and work. He always let me know I could come and talk to him anytime about anything. He constantly repeated that you are welcome to come to my office and talk. I would not and did not go to his office unless it was work-related and I did not have another choice. I did not care about those hints. I could handle it. I really thought after months of rejection that he would leave me alone, but I was wrong.

He became bold, intimidating, and more aggressive when he started putting his hands on me. I just could not take it anymore. I went into Captain Grace's office. I pulled out my little black book. I said Lt. Entitlement pressed his nose against my cheek and whispered to me "I'm going to lunch." I did not see it coming because he did it so fast. Five days later, he made the comment in front of Sgt. Naive and the Curriculum Coordinator (Janet) that I showed him how to download porn.

He put his arm around me and slid his hand down my back. Then, he fondled with my bra strap as though he was trying to unsnap it. I elbowed him very hard in his ribs; I mean I really gave him one. I knew that I hurt him because his chest caved in. My counter punch was to break his glasses but I caught myself. I know that I am a fighter and would have lost my job if I had broken his nose. I had been talking to Sgt. Naïve about Lt. Entitlement but I knew he did not have the constitution to say anything to him.

I was telling Janet about the incidents also because she was my friend. Lt. Entitlement put his arm around me that morning in front of Sgt. Naïve; I pulled away. I knew then I had to say something. If that elbow did not stop him, I knew we would eventually end up in a tussle or fight. April 28th, 2011, I filed sexual harassment against Lt. Entitlement (I had 16 years with the Sheriff's Dept.). Would you believe Lieutenant Entitlement was not only my supervisor but he taught the Sexual Harassment class at the Training Academy and on the Sexual Harassment Board, what a joke!

Everyone knew my reputation. I had never slept with any of them and they knew it. My word was my bond. If I said it happened, it happened. God knew I would have never said anything but he just would not stop.

The letter from the Bureau of Professional Standards and Integrity (BOPSI) stated that the investigation supported the conclusion that Lt. Entitlement did engage in the alleged conduct and violated policy and procedure. Therefore, the charges were sustained.

The administration moved Lt. Entitlement to Patrol right after I gave my statement. Do you know he kept coming to the Training Academy after they had reassigned him? I don't know why he continued to come to the Academy and speak to me. I told Captain Grace and he said well Mary, he can come to Training Academy. I said, he is not in class. He is not teaching any class. I felt that he was coming just to try to intimidate me, but it made me angry. I finally caught up with H.R. Manager Judy. Judy said, I did not know about that but she would check into it. I guess she did because he stopped the pop-up appearances.

After the sexual harassment charge, nobody would talk to me. Everyone avoided me like a plague. One Chief even got on his phone when he saw me coming in his direction. He wanted to be certain not to speak, God forbid, talk to me.

I was being harassed by someone working in the office at the Academy even after Administration moved Lt. Entitlement. My office name label came up missing three times. After the third time, I told the office Manager to just forget it. Someone went into my cubicle in my desk drawer and broke the strap on my new purse. This was just crazy. I put in a letter of transfer in December 2012 and left. By the way, administration wanted me to write in my transfer request that I was leaving because it was what I wanted to do and no other reason.

Do you know after all of this that before he retired, the Administration allowed him to come back and teach at the Training Academy? I was in In-Service class and he had the audacity to stand in front of me and ask me personally if I had any questions. I told him to get away from me. He also blocked my path as I was coming in the door. I pushed him very hard to the side and walked through. Until this day, I cannot wrap my mind around his behavior. I cannot grasp by any stretch of my imagination why the Administration would allow him to come back to the academy and teach under any circumstances. This is what the Administration created because they rewarded bad behavior. Lt. Entitlement enjoyed teaching at the training academy and they still gave him what he wanted to some extent.

The Administration subjected me to his harassment again. I felt humiliated, disrespected, disregarded and to say the least, insignificant. They gave him the green light condoning his bad behavior. I know for a fact that if I did not have concrete evidence against him they would have promoted him to captain. I guess that was supposed to be his disciplinary. The inequality of disciplinary action within the department is a topic that officers only talk about among themselves and this definitely should be looked into.

Lt. Entitlement finally retired; he emailed me a porn website. At this point, I was speechless. He was becoming a fatal attraction. I was raging mad when I went to BOPSI. If they had punished him in the first place, he would not have had the audacity to contact me in any way.

Commander Lucy continued to say I have known Lt. Entitlement for many years. He would not hurt you, he would not do anything to harm you in any way, and he is a nice guy and so on. I had to raise my voice at her because she was over-talking me. I said, Commander! You don't know him as a black woman! Listen to me and listen good! I am telling you today if we so happen to cross paths in some strange way and I fear for my life; "I will beat him livin!" (This was a saying from my Grandma Ruby).

"YOUR FRIEND OR FOE"

BEHIND THE SCENE

I knew if I filed Sexual Harassment charges against Lt. Entitlement that I would tarnish my career. I took all of that into consideration. I wanted him to just stop, but he had the mentality of entitlement towards black female officers and I could not get him to see otherwise. I blame some of the black female deputies for making it so easy for him which made it hell for me.

After filing my complaint, I was going back and forth to the Equal Employment Opportunity Commission (EEOC) in mediation meetings. Oh My God, I was stressed out to no end in sight. I had so many sleepless nights. I cried so much throughout the months. Deputy Lively caught me crying in my cubicle one evening. I thought everybody was gone for the day, but she never said anything to me about it. Also, I was going to school, studying, and taking care of my home. I continued to teach my classes and I knew everyone was talking about it.

I could not find a good Attorney. I did not know that the Attorney I hired was good friends with Chief Deputy Spade (Director Spade now has been promoted to Chief Deputy). The Attorney told me that Deputy Chief Spade told him I could sing and that he had my gospel CD. I was dumbstruck; there was no way I was going to tell him anything. That was his way of letting me know how close friends they were.

I found out Chief Deputy Spade and Director Lucy were good friends with Lt. Entitlement. Lt. Entitlement had been with the Sheriff's Office for I guess over thirty years with the other chiefs, directors, and commanders that were in charge. I was fighting a losing battle. Then to add insult to injury, Lt. Entitlement's father was a retired Chief from the Sheriff's Office in which I did not find out until later.

I did not know who I could trust so I did not talk to anyone about it. The investigation was kept within the Sheriff's Office. I realized later that I should have requested an outside investigation. I do not know if that would have happened. It seemed that everyone was long-term friends in the same circle.

I was going through a divorce and I did not want Lt. Entitlement to know. Some mornings my husband would take our daughter to school and sometimes he would not. Therefore, I allowed my sister and her children to move in with me. This was good because I did not have to worry about my daughter being at home alone. On the other hand, it had its issues because I still had to deal with other personalities in the house.

I was in school working on my bachelor's degree. So, I was sleep-deprived. I did not have a good diet and I was eating on the run. My school schedule was hectic; classes were 05:00 pm to 09:00 pm. I would get home from school, write papers or study. Sometimes I would get in bed at two and three in the morning. I went to school on Saturdays from 08:00 am to 05:00 pm, yes…all day.

I did not have school on Fridays and Sundays. I tried to spend time with my daughter but there was always homework to do and I was so tired. I was very active in my church teaching Sunday school, singing, and on the church board. I was burning the candle on both ends just as the old saying goes. My son BJ, an Officer in the United States Marine Corp, has a saying, "I Don't Know How to Quit!" I made up my mind that I was not going to quit. I graduated in 2013.

I had to pick the battle that I could win!

Share a time when you had difficulties balancing your career and personal life. What could you have done to make it better?

_____

_____

_____

_____

_____

BEHIND YOUR SCENE

I CHANGED

I should have ended up a basket case after these episodes in my life. We wonder why officers commit suicide, turn to alcohol and/or drugs, and have an increase in domestic violence. I could not find any recourse since everyone was afraid to help me. The Lieutenant that I thought was helping me was reporting back to his superiors. They had arterial motives to advance themselves, so I stopped talking to everybody.

I became focused and determined to win this battle. The biggest battle was within me. I could not take this personally. It was business. They were not going to let their longtime friend and partner go down in shame. I was just a casualty of his bad behavior. He was trying to crush me and the department was trying to make an example out of me; keep your mouth closed. Whether it was me or some other unimportant black female deputy, they were going to win. After being there for over fifteen years, I understood. Therefore, my battle was to graduate and I did. Sometimes perspective is everything. The big picture was not working for me. Therefore, I had to change the way I thought about it to survive.

While teaching at the Training Academy for four years, I don't think a week passed without at least one offer asking to go out on a date. The offers came from Chiefs down the chain of command to deputies. Chief Scooter and I would talk about the Bible quite often in his office. He said you know money is no object just name your price. He told me how his mother had so much land and she sold it and left him so much money and so on. I said, the Bible says that a good man leaves an inheritance to his children's children. Then, he said, you are a wise women. I do not think these come-ons were because I was so very attractive. I think it was because of my reputation. I had never dated any of them.

Name some officers you knew would do anything to get ahead. Have they ever made you a victim of their ambition? How and what did you do?

YOU'VE CHANGED

BELIEFS/CORE VALUES

I ask you these questions because I believe honest self-evaluation strengthens self-identification. It is very easy to see what you did but, in some instances, more difficult to explain why you did it. The naked eye cannot see motive in action. Motive has to be explained or discovered. I want you to assess yourself from beliefs/core values to understand who you are but most importantly why you are that way. As the phases in your career change, you change also. I want to help you identify the different phases and recognize how they changed you and why you made the changes. **If my experiences can help one officer live the best life in this career, I would have accomplished my mission.**

1) What is friendship to you? Are you that same friend to someone else?

_____

_____

_____

_____

_____

2) Do you find yourself thinking in private about how to turn every situation in your favor at any cost? Share

_____

_____

_____

_____

_____

3) Do you follow through on commitments? Share personal experiences when you have and when you have not and why.

_____
_____
_____
_____
_____
_____
_____

4) Do you know what your weaknesses are? Name some/why is it weakness?

_____
_____
_____
_____
_____
_____
_____

5) Do you know what makes you go from one to ten in a second? Name some/why?

_____

_____

_____

_____

_____

_____

_____

6) Do you know what your strengths are? Name some/why is it strength?

_____

_____

_____

_____

_____

_____

_____

_____

7) What have you given back during your career i.e., mentor rookies, community engagement?

_____
_____
_____
_____
_____
_____
_____

FUNCTION CIRCLES

Some days at work or even in our personal lives, we do not function at 100%. The circles represent your struggles. Sometimes you feel like you are walking on sunshine, other times the moon is laying on top of you; maybe you are pushing it along, and dragging it another day.

INSTRUCTIONS: Write your struggles in the circle and the characteristics that you are coping with during the time of your career. It is possible that you could have experienced more than one struggle at the same time? Write down that specific incident, how you actually coped with it, and how you changed.

1) **ME – My Health, Physical, Psychological, Emotional, Spiritual**

2) **PERSONAL LIFE** – Family, Friends, Finances, Love, Hate

3) **CO-WORKERS** – Trust, Secrets, Communication

4) **JOB** – Arrests, Overtime, Investigations, Injuries, Fights, Shootings, Deaths

5) **ADMINISTRATION** – Policy/Procedure, Evaluations, Reprimands, Fairness

There are more detailed characteristics you can write in the circles if you have experienced any of them during your career. For example:

Marriage/Separated/Divorce/Remarried/Relationships

Domestic-Violence/Drugs/Alcoholism

Children

Sick Family/Friend

Giving Statement to Internal Affairs

Post-Traumatic Stress Disorder (PTSD)

Sexual Harassment/Retaliation/Work Hostile Environment

Betrayal/Infidelity/Rumors

Testify in Court/Lawsuits

Suspended/Fired/Demoted

Stress/Duress

Report Writing

"WALKING ON SUNSHINE"

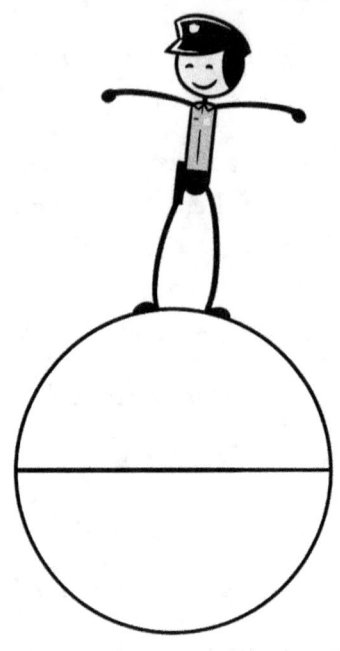

OPERATION POLICE PSYCHIC

"MOON LAYING ON YOU"

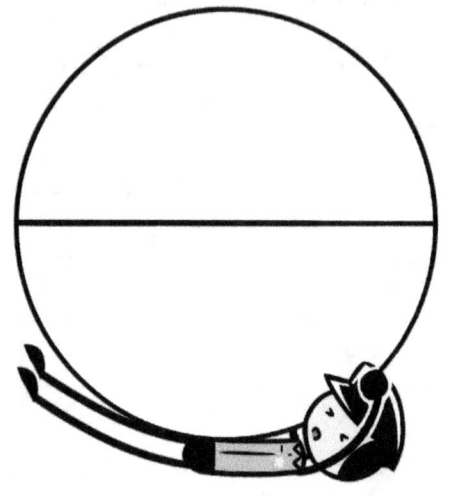

"PUSHING ON"

OPERATION POLICE PSYCHIC

"DRAGGING IN"

PHASE

III

CUT MY LOSES

How much longer can I do this job?

I was in this police career and ready to speed up the years. I tried to work overtime or get another job to payoff bills in order to have more money to invest. I was scrambling, trying to figure out how I was going to retire quicker and with more retirement money. I finally got to the point where it really did not matter.

Over the years, I have seen many officers come and go; some retired, some were fired, some moved on to bigger and better things. I regret saying this, but some officers committed suicide. You know the strangest thing since my retirement; I have not missed it even in the least bit. However, I do miss my friends.

When Captain Samson helped me get my job, he stated to me, "Mary, don't do anything to embarrass me or give me a bad name for vouching for you. I promised him that I would not but this job has many facets. Things happen out of your control and you are just stuck in the middle of it.

Name something an officer did and you were caught in the middle of it. What did you do and how did it change you.

_____

_____

_____

_____

_____

Discriminated Against In Uniform

Now, I am getting toward the end of my career and would you believe even in this day and time police officers in uniform still deal with racism. Deputy Flirty and I were partners and we stopped for lunch at this pizza place. I had never been there before so he led the way. He made his order; the cashier (female white) gave him a 50% discount. I was standing right behind him and we were in uniform, so I made my order and she charged me full price.

My partner said, she is a Deputy Sheriff so give her 50 % off her order! The young lady said it is too late I cannot change it. She offered me a big chocolate chip cookie. I didn't want that. I told him that's ok and I paid the full price. He was cussing and making a scene. I said don't worry about it this is not the first time this has happened. I never went back again.

Name a time you were discriminated against by citizens while you were on duty?

The last couple of years before I retired were very hard. Over the years, I thought maybe things would calm down for me but it just seemed as though I could not get away from ignorant people. In the Fugitive/Extradition Division, there was a television in the main work area. Two female deputies, Captain Bully and I were watching Family Feud.

I do not remember how we got on this particular subject. Captain Bully said, Mary, don't you fall asleep around here because "they" don't like you. He went on to say, "they" said if you fall asleep, they were going to choke you out. He put his hands together to demonstrate how to choke someone.

The black female Deputy Silky looked at me, her eyes said it all. She could not believe that he had just said that to me, especially in their presence (deputy Silky and I had been partners before in the same squad car). The white female Deputy Flat did not say a word. She actually pretended that she did not hear him. Captain Bully's desk was next to Deputy Flat and directly across from me (Captain Bully was known for his racist remarks and behavior). He later called a classroom of recruits some "porch monkeys" and nothing happened to him. His bad behavior is well known and accepted in the department, what a pitiful shame.

I stared at him eye to eye and said, "You go back and tell "they", whoever they are that I fear no man, I fear God. Now go back and tell they that." Captain Bully began to watch the Family Feud game with no response just like he had never said anything. Honestly, I was not afraid, I was just tired of fighting these personal attacks my entire career.

What do you think I did with that information from Captain Bully? Nothing! What could I do? He was a part of the "they" crew. If I had put that in writing, it would have created this whole mess of investigation that would have been conducted by his friends. I would have just created a bigger monster for myself. I had learned how to pick my battles and at this point, I did not care enough to fight.

Name some supervisors that were not worthy to wear this uniform?

_____

_____

_____

_____

_____

Leading up to my last major incident in my career happened in the Fugitive Extradition Division. The story goes like this. In October 2017, the runoff for Sheriff was going on. I had never campaigned for anyone in all of my twenty-plus years of service. However, I decided to support Chief Grace (Captain Grace from the Training Academy). He had retired from the Sheriff's Office years before he ran for Sheriff. We all knew each other in the campaign circles and who supported whom.

We all know that this is a very political job and if anyone says that it is not, they are not truthful. Since my candidate lost in 2018, of course, I knew I would suffer the consequences throughout the department under the new administration. What I mean by that is, suffer in some unfortunate way. No matter how much seniority I had in the department, the new administration would find a way to punish me; for example, placing me on the midnight shift or something. I figured I could retire in a year if things got too bad but that really was not my plan.

During the campaign, I was working in the Fugitive/Extradition Division; the office and break room area shared space. At the time, I was working with deputy Malicious in the Extradition Office. We were not on the best of terms before the results of the election.

Deputy Malicious was never at her desk. Therefore, she was not doing any work. I got so sick and tired of her coming to work late and eating breakfast in the break room or sometimes at her desk. She would take two-hour lunches and then still would not answer the phone while sitting at her desk. I did not care, however all of work was left for me to do. I complained about her never being at her desk to assist me with the workload, but my complaints fell on deaf ears.

Then Deputy Malicious and I had words in the break room in October 2017. I was trying to wait until she left the break room before I came in there for lunch but two hours had gone by and I was hungry. So I went into the break room and said to her, "are you watching this TV?" She said "Yes I am watching that" in a stern voice. I felt the tension from the way she responded. So I then replied, well you have been in here since 11:00 this morning and its 01:00 pm. She replied, "Who are you supposed to be, and why are you worried about how long I stay in the break room!"

I did not expect her to talk so loudly. She began ranting and raving so loud that other co-workers dodged across the doorway to see who she was talking to. I was not talking loud. I was in total control and I knew exactly what I was doing, aggravating her. I asked her, why are you talking so loud it's just me and you in here. She said I can talk how I want to and say what I want to say to you.

When tempers flared between you and another officer how did you handle that? After it was over did you forgive and move on? Did you continue to talk about it to other officers?

By this time Chief Sugar Daddy came into the break room and sat at the table with us. He asked, what is going on? Deputy Malicious said Mary came in here telling me how long I have been in the break room. I got up to warm my food in the microwave. She said, Mary is not my supervisor and she doesn't have any business coming to me about anything. *By the way, Deputy Malicious asked me to help her with her class assignments. She was in College for her Bachelor's Degree. I gave her my thumb drive and told her to get any assignment you need.*

I began to walk to the table from the microwave. I stopped in my tracks and said you know you are right. I said from now on if I have a complaint about you I will make it official and put it in writing. Chief Sugar Daddy said, Mary! I said no, I have tried to come to her and talk but she has proven to me that she is not that kind of woman.

So yes, after this I will put everything in writing although it didn't do any good. Lieutenant Goalong would not write her up, no supervisor would and they knew what she was doing. Lt Goalong was counting his days to retire. He did not care about anything. I couldn't blame him, nice guy though.

Oh but, after the election (August 2018), things got worse because Deputy Malicious' candidate won the office of Sheriff. All hell broke loose on me! We were walking in opposite directions in the hall and she intentionally bumped me shoulder to shoulder. I then walked straight out of the office and called a friend. I was so angry I had to walk down the street a block or two. Anyone who knows me knows that my voice carries with a loud punch. I was totally overwhelmed by the fact that she had the audacity to do that.

My friend said, go inside and write up the incident because you know yourself better than you know her. I know you and I don't want you to lose your job if she does anything else. You have to have something in writing, a paper trail. I felt like she was trying to bully me and put me in a position where I would have to defend myself. Now granted, I did not have a problem defending myself but under the circumstances with a new administration, I knew I would not be treated fairly. Therefore, I went back inside and wrote up the incident. I sent the write-up to Lieutenant Naïve and Captain Lefty.

I took off work for a few days after the incident. When I returned that Thursday, Lieutenant Naïve handed me a letter stating that I was reassigned to the Civil Division. I was not upset about going back there as much as I was the reason I was being sent back. I was upset about the principle of the matter, retaliation. She intentionally bumped into me and I was moved. I did not want to go back out to the streets; I had more seniority than she did. Lieutenant Naïve said to me, I don't understand but my hands are tied. I did not blame him; he was just following orders just like Lieutenant Goalong. It was retaliation, they knew it and I was livid.

What did you do when the disappointment in a decision or person was overwhelming? Did you seek revenge?

_____

_____

_____

_____

_____

_____

_____

_____

_____

_____

If you think that was bad. This was not the worst of it. I really wanted to work back at the desk. I was 53 years old and after twenty-plus years, I really wanted to get out of the streets. So I got an anonymous phone call that Extradition had an open position since Deputy Malicious went to work in courts. So of course, I made some phone calls to inquire just to make sure it was legit.

By this time the Fugitive Division had a different Chief. I had gotten along with Chief O'Riley in the past and we did not have any problems that I knew of. I talked with Chief O'Riley and he assured me that I would get that desk position in the Extradition Department. So I wrote the transfer request memo and sent it in.

Officer Stable, one of my best friends and partners kept telling me over and over to stay your ass here. He said don't go back over there where you are not wanted. I was telling him this is a different Chief and we get along just fine. I had already talked to him and he was so cool. If you know politics, it is just a circle of lots of information, misinformation and outright lies. One must be able to decipher what is what and sometimes it is hard to do depending on who says it and what is being said. Chief O'Riley called me and said I got your letter of transfer and everything looks good.

I called an anonymous friend and we were just having a casual conversation about coming back over there to work. He said I heard that you are going back in the streets in the Fugitive Division. I said no, I just talked with Chief O'Riley and that is not what he told me. He made the statement that he overheard a conversation about me and that I was being put on Baker Shift in the streets. The turn of events was spinning quickly so I had to chase it down.

I immediately called Chief O'Riley back and asked him if he was planning to put me in Fugitive on Baker Shift in the streets. He replied, well yes Mary. I said why would you do that? You know I wanted to go to a desk position otherwise I would have stayed where I am. He said well I need boots on the ground right now so I had to put you where I needed you. We are short in the Fugitive Division and I need officers in the streets. So I had to make some changes.

I said that the Sheriff's office is short-staffed everywhere so that is no big deal. I said so you deliberately deceived me?! I thought we were better than that Chief O'Riley. He said maybe we can work out something, for instance, alternate the desk some nights. Suggesting something crazy like that, at that point you know I did not believe anything he said. I truly felt helpless and betrayed.

Have you been in a situation in the department and felt hopeless? What did you do?

_____

_____

_____

_____

_____

_____

_____

_____

_____

So, I made another phone call to a dear friend of mine Deputy Willhite. He advised me to call Chief Deputy Sugar Daddy who is Chief Inspector and O'Riley's supervisor. Well, Chief Sugar Daddy was the same that reassigned me to the Civil Division in the first place. Yes, the same Chief that sat in the break room during the misunderstanding with Deputy Malicious. I called him and at this point what did I have to lose? I had him on speaker so my husband could hear the conversation. I explained what happened as though he did not already know. I knew that he was the culprit behind this charade all along. You know I couldn't very well say that.

He was still salty about his businesses being exposed with his little boo thang. I said, I have been here twenty 24 years and I am 53 years old and you are going to put me in the streets? How could you! Are you trying to get me killed? He didn't respond; we heard crickets. He said absolutely nothing! I realized then this was more serious to him than I had grasped. The person I thought I knew all of these years I really did not know at all. His heart was revealed to me and it was frightening. He did not say I would never want anything to happen to you or any officer on my watch. He said NOTHING!

Have you known officers for many years and they changed? You thought you knew them but you found out you did not know them at all; how did you handle that?

Chief Inspector O'Riley called me back and asked me did you call Chief Sugar Daddy? I said yes sir. He said why? Why did you do that? I cannot believe you called him! So now you know he is livid. He said, you do not tell me where you are going to work you understand? I said yes sir. He said I will see you Monday at 14:00 hours! I said yes sir.

That conversation was on a late Friday evening at about 8:00 pm. So you know that I was on the phone for four days trying not to go back to Fugitive Baker Shift in the streets knocking on doors at night. All of this started on a Wednesday afternoon when I wrote the transfer letter and ended with Chief O'Riley Saturday afternoon.

I don't know what happened. I do know that God answered my prayer. From that conversation on Friday evening, Chief O'Riley gave me a direct order to report to Fugitive Baker Shift. Until the conversation on Saturday afternoon, God moved on his heart. Maybe Chief O'Riley decided not to do Chief Sugar Daddy's dirty work.

Chief O'Riley said Mary, we have always gotten along. I said yes sir. He said I don't know what happened but you can stay where you are. You have been here a long time, you have always been a hard worker and you have enough seniority to at least work where you like.

I responded, Chief I was going to show up Monday ready to do my job and you would not have heard anything else about this incident. He said I know because that is just the God-fearing woman you are. He said, I discussed with Chief Inspector Davis (he is the supervisor over the Civil Division) and we decided to allow you to stay where you wanted. I said thank you Chief.

About a week and half later, Sergeant Easy, my immediate supervisor, called me into his office. He said I was given orders to write you up. I said yeah I know. Where is it? I'll sign it. He said you don't even know what it is about. I replied, yes I do. Sergeant Easy said I don't understand what happened. I said I do. I read the negative Observation Behavior Report (OBR) and then I laughed. He said what is so funny? I told him just enough to get the idea. Basically, I was written up for jumping the chain of command. I told Sergeant Easy yes, I did it.

I explained to Sergeant Easy that I had been talking directly to Chief O'Riley from the beginning of this move. I wrote my transfer request letter to move back to Fugitive in the Extradition Office directly to him. If I had not spoken directly to him about working in Extradition at the desk, I would have never written the transfer request.

Once I found out that they were planning to put me in Fugitive on Baker Shift back in the streets I called him. Once he admitted it was true, I called his supervisor Chief Deputy Sugar Daddy.

I think they forgot that they were actually dealing with a seasoned veteran officer and that I was not afraid of any of them. I respected their position but not really them as a man that is earned. I was not disrespectful to them but I was not afraid to speak up for myself. I mean at this point what was the worst that could happen. Plus, I was just downright sick of the whole game playing with my life so I went straight to the sources.

Describe a time you came to a breaking point that you did not care about the repercussions and decided to stand up and speak up?

_____

_____

_____

_____

_____

_____

_____

Over twenty years ago when I was hired, Chief Inspector O'Riley was an officer and he was wild and funny. He fought for the underdogs. Chief Deputy Sugar Daddy was an easy-going Sergeant and very pleasant to be around. I never thought in a million years that he would have turned out to be this way in the latter years of his career. Chief Sugar Daddy was the bitter man behind all of this. Reading the negative OBR, his name was all over it. Captain Dabble was following direct orders. This was business, not personal.

There was something more colossal going on behind all of this. I had no idea. You know there are no secrets in the Sheriff's Office and everybody knows somebody's business. Most of the time you do not know who is related to whom and who knows who is in related in an intimate way.

Word got back to me that Captain Dabble followed up with Lieutenant Stern to inquire about the write-up on me. Well, she said, I told Sergeant Easy to write up a negative OBR on her. Captain Dabble was livid about Lieutenant Stern's response. He said, I told you to write her up a reprimand. A reprimand would have stayed in my personal file and followed me to another Division in the Sheriff's office for at least a year. They said Capt. Dabble hung up the phone and called back a few minutes later. He asked Lt. Stern, did Mary sign the negative OBR? Lieutenant answered yes sir she signed it.

Name some supervisors that stood up for you or protected you?

_____

_____

_____

_____

If I had not signed that negative OBR, then he could have given her a direct order to write up a reprimand. Little did I know that once I signed that negative OBR, there was nothing else they could do, that finalized the paperwork?

On the other hand, if I had gotten reprimanded, any transfer assignments I wanted or promotions coming up could have been denied. You see, I had taken the Sergeant Test and I scored better than most this time around. It was a possibility that I could have been up for promotion. He knew that kind of reprimand would disqualify me from any chance of advancement.

Have you had someone in your department who just haunted you like prey? It appeared that their entire career was making certain you did not get any kind of advancement. How did you cope with it? How did that make you feel?

_____

_____

_____

_____

_____

_____

After all of these years, I was too happy. I was not disgruntled, bitter or complaining about anything. I accepted the fact that I was going to retire a slick sleeve, which meant no promotion. I had my dignity and self-respect and I was going to run with it. Sergeant Rogers told me all you have to do is make someone very happy. I knew what that meant. I knew if I had sex with one, he would have told the others and the **pass around** would have been their next move. I didn't like them enough to give them my peace of mind and **more importantly, I feared God.** It seems as though I was ostracized for trying to do the right thing.

What is most important to you, the money and status or your self-respect and dignity? Share some of the times you have had to choose. Share moments when you compromised.

_____
_____
_____
_____
_____
_____
_____
_____
_____
_____
_____

Finally, I had had enough so I took the advice of a veteran officer who had retired about seven years before me. Deputy Advice once told me just before he retired, "Mary, always keep at least six months of vacation and sick time on the books; they might put you somewhere you don't want to work then you can burn some time."

***Sidebar** - Deputy Advice and I worked in the Civil Field Division. We went to a young lady's house to serve papers. She opened the door so we asked her if we could come inside. She said yes, so we helped her push the door open so we could come in. There were clothes behind the door, all over the floor and everywhere. I was explaining to her what the papers were about.*

I looked at my partner and he was shaking his foot. He was on the other side of the coffee table so I could not see. He was not saying anything but he had his hands in his coat pockets and shaking, shaking, shaking that one foot. So, when we got back to the squad car, I said what is wrong with you? He said her red panties were stuck under the bottom of my boot and I couldn't shake'em off. Oh, I laughed until I cried. We laughed the rest of the day and I could not wait to tell the fellas.

Not all of our experiences are bad; tell something funny that has happened to you in the field?

_____

_____

_____

_____

_____

_____

_____

I begin to burn time. I used Family Medical Leave (FMLA) taking a little here and there. The doctor said I have arthritis, especially in my hands. When I went to the doctor, he asked me how many times I have broken my thumbs. My response was I didn't know I had broken them. I fell forward coming up some icy stairs in 2018. I caught myself in a push-up position and jammed both my wrist. After that, my thumbs and wrists would lock and it was so painful.

I eventually got cortisone shots in both wrists. I have had knee injections, three shots in each knee. My back even gives me the blues sometimes but I refused to allow anyone do anything to it. Over the years, the gun belt with all of the bells and whistles, the bullet-proof vest, boots and other gear, wears and tears on the physical body.

I have not mentioned the mental battle scars from the administration and also the streets. This job is **STRESSFUL** on all sides and we also have our personal lives to balance through all of it.

Share some of your mental and physical aches and pains because of this job.

_____

_____

_____

_____

_____

_____

_____

_____

Now, I am at the point to retire, although it was not my plan. I took off work in July of 2019 because I was burnt out. I needed a mental break. I came back to work after about two or three weeks. I thought I was just in my emotions but when I got into that squad car, I couldn't do it anymore. I prayed, Lord if it is meant for me to retire, I need to know beyond a shadow of a doubt. I could not retire in good conscience without being absolutely certain it was time.

I had just bought a car and had only driven it for about seven days. There I was at 05:00 a.m. taking my things out of my personal vehicle putting them in the squad car. I looked up at my drive-out tags and it read **QUTJ2U7:**

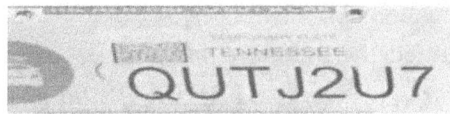

I sat down in my squad car for about twenty minutes. I could not believe what I was looking at so I took a picture of it. At that moment, a certain type of fear came over me. The fear of God, that He heard me, answered so quickly and that He loved me that much.

My interpretation of the drive-out tag: **QUT-quit, J-job, 2-to, U-you, 7-God's perfect number** it is completed.

Quit job to you God said it is completed!

As soon as the Retirement Office opened at 08:00 am, I was there putting in my paperwork. I had already inquired about it weeks before I bought the car. I thought to myself I had not properly prepared to retire like most officers. Believing God, I put the papers in anyway. Afterwards, I felt a sense of relief.

Lieutenant Stern asked me if she could tell Chief Sugar Daddy that I was retiring. I told her no Ma'am, he does not like me like that. So, for some odd reason, she just continued to ask me if she could tell him. I said yes against everything in me, I told her yes anyway.

I came in after the shift to put up my equipment. Lt. Stern asked me to come into her office. I went in and closed the door. She said to me what did you do to him? I have known him for over thirty years and he has never talked about anyone the way he talked about you. I replied, I have not done anything to Chief Sugar Daddy.

It may be what I have not done that makes him so angry. Also, I think he is bitter because I wrote up his boo thang. Then he reassigned me back over here, everyone knew he was messing around with her. The upstanding Deacon in the church and Sunday school teacher; I guess all of this may have tarnished his reputation. I don't know and at this point, I don't care.

I made the statement to Lieutenant Stern that I was going to take off all of August. She went back and told Chief Sugar Daddy. He blew a gasket. I received a phone call from Sergeant Rogers. He said you have to have a doctor's statement to take off August. I replied, yes sir. He said Mary, you know who this is coming from, I said yes sir. He said so please as soon as you can bring in the doctor's statement. I said yes sir. I got you covered don't worry about it. He called me again with the same conversation.

Mary, please have the doctor's statement on Monday. I said, yes sir. He said Chief Sugar Daddy is riding Lt. Stern and she is calling me. I said Sarge I got you. He said I know but she has called me several times. I said to him I am going to call Lieutenant to ease her mind. (You see, Lt. had already had a stroke and has been back to work maybe a year. Chief Sugar Daddy was stressing her out and he did not care about her health).

I called Lt. Stern and told her I will have the doctor's statement on Monday although my appointment is late that afternoon but don't worry I got you. She said, Mary if you do not have that doctor's statement, I have direct orders to take your vacation hours instead of your sick hours.

To make you understand how significant this information was, let me explain. When Deputies retire, we are paid for all vacation hours, accumulated and bonus hours. On the other hand, no matter how many sick hours we have, we only are paid 75 of them. All of this was contingent on how much we made annually and I knew my income was more than they required. Chief Sugar Daddy was deliberate and calculating, forcing Lt. Stern to use my vacation time. He was still very angry, bitter and revengeful towards me. I was disturbed and needless to say, very angry.

I talked to Lt. Stern on the phone most of the way home. After we ended the call, I cried and prayed the rest of the way. I pulled up into the garage crying and came in the house crying. No one was home, I was so overwhelmed I could barely catch my breath. I heard my husband and daughter come into the house later, but I could not talk. I was so distraught. Finally, I calmed down and I told my husband they won't leave me alone. I said, they wanted me gone so now I'm leaving. I felt like they wanted me to leave wounded for life. I just did not understand how someone could hold grudges and seek revenge at any cost. I knew I was never coming back to work.

Honestly, I asked myself am I such a horrible person? I had not done anything to deliberately hurt Chief Sugar Daddy or anyone for that matter. I felt like I was actually getting away from some kind of monster that would not let me go and almost caught me in the end.

I left on my terms and I think that infuriated him more, this was my conclusion.

Later on that same Friday evening, Captain Crunch called me. (I cannot make this stuff up, I am not that good). I thought he was my friend. When I heard his voice I knew immediately that it was a set-up. I knew that Chief Sugar Daddy was on the phone. I could not prove it but I had that gut feeling. I said what's up Otis? He said hey Mary how are you doing? I said Captain, I can't do this anymore. I feel like when I get in the squad car the walls are closing in on me. I don't feel right. I can't think straight. Right now I am a liability if I come to work, right?

He's been my good friend for many years. He said, okay Mary take care. As a Captain, he was supposed to report what I said. He could have either passed this information down to Lieutenant Stern to get some paperwork started on me, or he was supposed to start the paperwork himself to get me some help. He did not ask me, Mary is there anything I can do? I am sorry you are going through this, how can I help? He did not ask do you need anything or take as much time as you need, I will check on you tomorrow to see how we can work this out no, **nothing!**

He did not say any words of consideration or consultation – how cruel, I thought. I don't take it personally though. Its business and it was time for him to pay back a favor. Politicians have dirt on each other and when it is time to pay back a favor, it's time. I was just a casualty of the game. I have not seen or heard from him since. I don't play the game of politics but I know the rules of engagement to survive.

Did he think I was going to say, oh yeah Captain I am taking off sick in August to burn some time? Why not? I had the time and everybody does it, right? Well for me, Chief Sugar Daddy would have had a heart attack before he allowed me to burn sick time. I don't know what he had planned but God would not allow it. Amen!

WIN OR LOSE

BEHIND THE SCENE

This is an example of my life behind the scene. I was transferred back to the Civil Division serving papers to the public in August of 2018. I remember it so well because it was when my Aunt passed. I was at work on Friday morning around 11:00 am when I finally thought to check on my aunt. I talked to her for about 10 minutes, not long because her voice sounded so weak. She said, thank you for checking on me. I replied you don't have to thank me for that. She said yes I do. She passed away that same day at approximately 10:30 pm on August 10th, 2018.

I got back to work on Monday still trying to grapple with the reality that I spoke to my aunt the same day she died. I came out of the bathroom crying and just trying to pull myself together. As I came out of the bathroom, Deputy Malicious turned that corner and we caught each other's eyes. I intentionally moved over to the wall because the hallway was narrow.

Without a doubt, deputy Malicious intentionally walked into my space and bumped my right shoulder hard enough to push my momentum backward. I was already dealing with the death of my aunt. I wanted to oblige her in that challenge, but I knew I would have lost because of the new administration. In politics/bureaucracy, it is always business and I was too close to retirement to throw it all away on someone that really didn't matter to me at that time.

Another stressing family ordeal was our daughter. She was a senior in high school. She came home crying most of her senior year because she was being bullied in school. She pleaded and begged us not to go to the administration because she feared that the children would become even more angry and aggressive towards her, so we respected her reasoning. We told her, "Go to school with your head up and do not let them see you cry." Thank God none of them put their hands on her but they threatened her on videos. I just did not see this coming to the point where my daughter was being bullied. Oh My God, this was stressful!

Of course, we all know there are lots of expenses – senior events, graduation and preparing for college. So that was another stressful factor going on in my life behind all of the drama at work.

When we are stressed and pressured, we have to have an outlet whether constructive or destructive. So, I had therapy just about every morning during the last year of my career working in the Civil Field. Deputy Stable (partner and friend) and I would go to our favorite spot, the Easy-Train Gas Station, for coffee. We met our morning crew there ready to cut up. I called the cashier Easygoing, Mr. Uptight cleaned up around the station, and then there was Shady, who made everybody laugh. He called me Angel (like the show Charlie's Angels).

Sly was really cool like old school but still keeping up with the young guys. Cool was smooth but funny and always had some words of wisdom. The Cooking crew over the years was Ms. Sadie, Ms. Sassy and Simmy. The customers going in and out were like family. We would talk about the news, politics, church, or whatever was trending at the time, nothing was off-limits. We didn't know a stranger but strange things happened and strangers would show up every now and then. We would laugh and have the best times all in love. I miss those days more than anything else. That kind of therapy was the best and it was free.

What is your therapy at work or after work?

_____

_____

_____

_____

_____

_____

Through it all, I never got promoted no matter how I qualified for the job. I was a firearms instructor through Federal Bureau Investigation (FBI) training. I was a physical fitness instructor. I taught Emergency Vehicle Operations (EVO). I was passionate about teaching. I eventually got my Master's Degree in Criminal Justice. If that was not enough, nothing was!

What was something that you made peace within yourself about in order to move forward without anger?

BEHIND YOUR SCENE

I CHANGED

When we change our WHY, everything else changes too.

I have seen so many officers become angry and bitter working in law enforcement. Officers wh o are underappreciated become slothful and unconcerned and this can be dangerous for them and others. This job is challenging from the administration side, working with your partners and actually doing the job in the field. An officer's morale can become low – sometimes very low.

Sometimes we can work with officers that like to push the envelope and do things that are questionable, illegal or right at the brink of breaking the law. The decision to stand against this kind of behavoir is not popular and sometimes you will be labeled, like I was. This is when you have to establish who you are and where you stand within yourself, your partner and the department.

Are you a disgruntled officer? Do you complain about the smallest things? Why? When did it start?

_____
_____
_____
_____
_____
_____
_____
_____

I was disrespected by the department as a whole. I was in survival mode, nevertheless I can say I survived. I asked God to let me walk away from the department the way I walked in and He did. There were so many other fights and struggles that I had within the Sheriff's Office far too many to tell. After I realized that I was never going to be promoted no matter how much I was qualified, I relented.

Every officer needs to have a plan B and this mindset needs to be taught in recruit school.

Have you discovered that the urge in your heart to speak up about injustices in the department has dissipated? What was the deciding factor?

_____

_____

_____

_____

_____

After all, there is a point in your career when it is just time to go and when that time comes, please leave. Do not stay too long after your warnings because this can be very detrimental for you. I know that you have heard stories of officers being killed right before retirement or getting seriously injured. There have been many instances were officers died six months to a year after they retire which is so heartbreaking.

I had an officer tell me "I stayed too long." He said, I had been on the department forty-two years and I felt that I should have been gone. But, I was afraid I didn't have anywhere else to go." After he was seriously

OPERATION POLICE PSYCHIC

injured in a fight, he left. I saw him in the grocery store after he had been retired for some years. He said, "I should have left a long time ago. I am working, remarried, and having the time of my life." Do not give this career everything; save some part of yourself to enjoy life afterwards. Sometimes I think about how I made such a great sacrifice for such a rewarding but thankless job.

Please name some officers that lived only a short time (six months to five years) after retirement. Name officers that could have retired, but decided to stay, got injured, and was forced to retire. Name officers that have said I do not have anything else to do if I retire.

_____

_____

_____

_____

_____

_____

_____

_____

_____

I have seen police officers, deputy sheriffs and jailers' personalities change during their careers. Sometimes we lose our way in this job. I just refused to be a pass-around or a puppet.

I did not get the big retirement pension that I desired.

That was the price I paid to leave with my DIGNITY and SELF-RESPECT!

There is this code of silence that we understand. We know if we bring embarrassment to the Department, they will cast us out of the fold. They will ignore our calls and our presence. Some officers cannot cope with the isolation especially when they have made this job their identity. I was talking with a deputy that had gotten into some trouble. He said to me, I will kill myself if they fire me. They did not fire him but this is the mindset of some of our officers that lose their way. Do not allow anyone to hold you hostage because you want more for yourself. In other words, never want anything so bad until you are willing to do anything to get it.

When I taught at the academy, I would always tell the recruits this is not your life but your livelihood. I would encourage them to continue to stay connected to their outside friends, family, faith-based communities, and hobbies. I have had knee injections and the doctor said I have arthritis in my back. Some days my back hurt so badly that I could barely walk. Officers have had knee and hip replacements over their careers. I am certain this is from all of the gear we carry over the years. Also, statistics show that officers have a high rate of divorce, suffer from Post-Traumatic Stress Disorder (PTSD), an increased rate of suicide and have a shorter life span after retirement than many other careers.

Our performance on the job changes because yes, we change. That is not saying that we do not do a good job because we do. Sometimes we even do it better. As officers, we just need to understand who we are and why we are this way. Understanding yourself is the key to being a better person and officer.

YOU'VE CHANGED

BELIEFS/CORE VALUES

I ask you these questions because I believe honest self-evaluation strengthens self-identification. It is very easy to see what you did but, in some instances, more difficult to explain why you did it. The naked eye cannot see motive in action. Motive has to be explained or discovered. I want you to assess yourself from beliefs/core values to understand who you are but most importantly, why you are that way. As the phases in your career change, you change also. I want to help you identify the different phases and recognize how they changed you and why you made the neccessary changes. **If my experiences can help one officer live the best life in this career, I would have accomplished my mission.**

1) What are you passionate about and how does it drive your success?

_____

_____

_____

_____

_____

2) Do you commit yourself to be a better person and how? What are your personal self-growth plans? How do you implement them into your life every day?

_____

_____

_____

_____

_____

3) What are your greatest fears? Name some/why?

4) What are your greatest joys? Name some/why?

5) Do you believe your word is your bond? Why?

6) Do you believe keeping your word to yourself is more important than keeping it to someone else? Why or why not?

_____

_____

_____

_____

_____

_____

UNDERSTANDING

A Deputy Sheriff was killed in a motorcycle accident. So I bided for his position for the midnight fugitive shift working the desk because that was best for me and my family at the time. Officer Grief was his partner and they worked together for many years. Officer Grief was unfriendly and would not talk to me unless it was work-related. I knew he was grieving the loss of his partner. So I wrote him a poem. After I gave him the poem, it relieved the tension between us and we could work together better.

"I Find Myself"

Taking a person's position never means taking their place.

The position I qualify for,

The position that gives me more,

The position that works for me,

The position I have to be,

A place that has taken you years to build,

A place where memories are revealed,

A place in your heart concealed,

A place that cannot be filled.

by: Mary Caldwell Evans

CONCLUSION

POLICE OFFICERS and FIRST RESPONDERS change over the years in their careers. **I know that I changed.** Some of my changes were good, some not so good and some were bad. I tried not to allow the changes to affect my job but is this even possible? The job tested my integrity, core values and beliefs. There was a constant self-reevaluation and job examination to scrutinize my motives. There must be more case studies on first responders to understand how the job affects us and the effects on our decisions.

Research is important to the Criminal Justice System because of the danger to police officers, their partners, the general public, and other governmental departments. Therefore, the problems of law enforcement and the adverse effects on the officer must be recognized and addressed in order to develop preventive measures and to offer assistance to officers, before burnout and undue stress (Violanti, 1999).

Unhealthy lifestyle behaviors including poor to little physical fitness, sedentary habits, and poor nutrition each play a role in increased stress, beyond the duties associated with being a police officer, and contribute to a reduced life expectancy of an officer. Poor nutrition, inadequate sleep, sleep disturbances, and coping with situations could lead to negative behaviors, such as excessive drinking and tobacco usage that also contribute to an officer's decreased life expectancy (Tanigoshi, Holly, Kontos, Remley & Theodore, 2008).

Everyone has different education, life experiences, rules of conduct, and moral principles that make us who we are. No matter what you are going through personally, you must apply your skills, training and knowledge for the best outcome. This book was created out of the need for officers to be fully aware of their mindset, which influences their decisions more than any training, policy, and procedure.

On the other hand, when we as officers make a decision in good faith and it still goes south, it is important that we do not beat ourselves up about it over and over. You know within your heart that you did what was best under the circumstances with the information given. Forgive yourself. We can "what if" a situation to no end, but the only thing that changes is time and information. I know that officers are taught to be fair, firm and consistent but remember that we must also have that human touch called compassion. Therefore, let our decisions be sound, honest, without prejudices or biases, then let it go.

Police Reformation is desperately needed but very difficult to achieve because it starts from the inside out of the officers and from the top to the bottom of the Department. It has been much easier to create combative strategies when the enemy is someplace else. However, when the enemy is right in your house it is very, very difficult to reform. Superiors must do due diligence to serve justice for all people; that includes accountability to the officers, community engagement, and transparency to the public.

Now Law Enforcement Agencies have come to what may be the hardest test ever and that is to implement and follow through on <u>CHANGING THE MINDSET</u> of their Officers and Administrators.

However, YOU must not and YOU cannot depend on the Administration to do what you can do for yourself. Now you are equipped to change yourself, help a partner, precinct, division, department, administration, and city all one at a time! Since you have had time to think about your experiences, go out and help a fellow officer! Don't be afraid to share your experiences no matter how vulnerable it makes you appear.

<u>MOST OF US ARE THE GOOD GUYS!</u>

I Truly Believe in YOU!
BELIEVE IN YOURSELF!

NOTES:

OPERATION POLICE PSYCHIC

REFLECTIONS:

OPERATION POLICE PSYCHIC

REFERENCE

Tanigoshi, H., Kontos, A., & Remley, T. (2008). The effectiveness of individual wellness counseling on the wellness of law enforcement officers. *Journal of Counseling and Development*. Retrieved from: http://search.proquest.com/docview/

219030066/ 1391CE36511FD03/2?accountid=40

Ussery, W. & Waters, J. (2007). Police Stress: History, contributing factors, symptoms, and interventions.*Criminology and Law Enforcement*. Retrieved from http://search.proquest.com/docprintview/ 211

Violanti, M. J. (1999). Alcohol Abuse in Policing Prevention Strategies. *The FBI Law Enforcement Bulletin*.

BIOGRAPHY

WWW.OPERATIONPOLICEPSYCHIC.COM

MARY CALDWELL EVANS was born in Pine Bluff, Arkansas, moved to St. Louis, Missouri in 1971 and then to Memphis, Tennessee in 1978 and now resides in Southaven, MS. She is married to Bobby Evans Sr. and they have three adult children: Robert, Bobby Jr. and Myr-acle as well as one teenage grandson, Kendall. She is the eighth child of eleven children, three brothers and seven sisters. She loves to journal, write poems, and sing songs. She challenges herself to new exciting adventures. Her greatest joy in life is helping people become the best they can be.

She retired from the Shelby County Sheriff's Department in 2019. Mary was an Instructor at the Shelby County Training Academy for four years. She taught all levels of Law Enforcement from Chiefs to recruits. A graduate of Bethel University in McKenzie, Tennessee with her Masters of Science Degree in Criminal Justice in 2015 and a graduate of LeMoyne-Owen College in Memphis, Tennessee with a Bachelors of Arts Degree in Criminal Justice in 2013.

Mary has Instructor Development Certification through the Shelby County Training Academy, Memphis, TN. She is a Firearm's Instructor; she acquired her Certification from the Federal Bureau of Investigation (FBI) of Memphis, TN. She has Combat Shooting Certification from Tom Long Desoto County, MS. She has Certifications from The Institute of Law Enforcement Administration Dallas, TX - Police Media Relations and Ethics Train-The-Trainer. She has Certifications from Tennessee Law Enforcement Training Academy (TLETA), Nashville, TN - Courtroom Security, Child Sex Abuse, and Emergency Vehicle Operation (EVO).

MY PRAYER:

Dear Lord God, I pray for all police, firefighters, military, first responders, jailers, and the personnel that support first responders and essential workers. May God keep you whole, of sound mind, safe, and healthy as you prosper. God bless you to have the courage to change when it is time and thrive in your career. Give you fairness in representation from Administrations, Unions, and Courtrooms. Lord God, bless them to know when it's time to take leave, resign or retire and give them the courage to do so. Strengthen their coping mechanisms through constructive behaviors. As they put their lives on the line to serve and protect others, Father I pray that You take care of their loved ones as well. Unify the Law Enforcement Agencies from the Administration to the Officers to the People, brings us together because we all need each other to survive.

In Jesus Mighty Name, Amen!

PSALMS 41:11-13 By this I know that thou favourest me, because mine enemy doth not triumph over me. And as for me, thou upholdest me in mine integrity and settest me before thy face for ever. Blessed be the Lord God of Israel from everlasting, and to everlasting, Amen, and Amen.

Interested in Writing and or Publishing Your Own Book??? Visit

www.A2ZBookspublishing.net

www.ingramcontent.com/pod-product-compliance
Lightning Source LLC
Chambersburg PA
CBHW071457070526
44578CB00001B/374